SONGS OF HANNIBAL

Homesongs, Sensual Love Poems
& Other Works
(Including Selections from
Boyhood in Hannibal)

JOSEPH WELCH

Tampa, Florida

This book is a work of fiction. The names, characters and events in this book are the products of the author's imagination or are used fictitiously. Any similarity to real persons living or dead is coincidental and not intended by the author.

Songs of Hannibal: Homesongs, Sensual Love Poems & Other Works (Including Selections from *Boyhood in Hannibal*)

Published by Gatekeeper Press
7853 Gunn Hwy, Suite 209
Tampa, FL 33626
www.GatekeeperPress.com

Library of Congress Control Number: 2023935679

ISBN (hardcover): 9781662936616
ISBN (paperback): 9781662936623
eISBN: 9781662940163

"Since Love is lord of heav'n and earth,
How can I keep from singing?"

      — Anonymous

"I thank all who have loved me in their hearts,
With thanks and love from mine. Deep thanks to all
Who paused a little near the prison-wall
To hear my music in its louder parts
Ere they went onward....Oh, to shoot
My soul's full meaning into future years,
That they should lend it utterance, and salute
Love that endures, from life that disappears!"

     — *Sonnets from the Portuguese*
      Elizabeth Barrett Browning

Acknowledgments

Thanks to Hannibal's preeminent commercial drone pilot, Dave Hirner, and his lovely and talented wife, Paula, Owners of Flying Squirrel Aerial Optics, who furnished the fabulous cover photography.

To Sharon, my muse
And to Eric, Christopher, Colin, Maria & Theresa,
our joyous, loving and generous children,
and their families

Table of Contents

The House That Dad Built

When I was young enough to swim in my yard
on a hot summer afternoon in Hannibal
in the old not-so-galvanized steel washtub

feeling with my toes the rusty dents on the bottom
and always maintaining out of a certain caution
a heavy sheen of water on the scorched sides

I loved from trust and example
the man who cut our grass
and built a big sandbox around the elm

with six different seats
in six different corners
for his six different sons.

Homesong

Only a good morning's walk downriver
might bring any traveler
to the top of a bluff
overlooking an island
where bald eagles winter,
wrapped in eagledown
all but the eyes,
and on the same road along the bluffs
hawks might be seen
dipping and gliding
and diving through the humid air.

And a friend's house
(because once, thirsty
on a bicycle, I drank
from his spigot,
and another summer
he offered my brother
a piece of watermelon)
though I don't know his name
I always bless his house in passing.

Perhaps because of this
I have found the scent of
honeysuckle in Hannibal
to overwaft fine Kentucky bourbon,
heavy on the lips and sultry in the eyes
and perhaps because of other things:

onetwothree on Linda
       still
if the Harriets are gone or going
there are some Henrys yet
and Marks
but Mark will always be
a part of Hannibal--an effluent
like the great river
come again   gone
but not unfelt
like the Bear Creek morning mist
crowning down our valley
through all our bones;

the maiden crop
softer and sweeter from thirteen to sixteen
with toys in the heads
                    unformed yet
to tools and the city's dreams--
enough cars and meat and diplomas
to list and stamp with jade.

So unpin and drop in any cowpath
this restless suit;
lay it unsought and uninquired by the hooved traffic
that the wind of my home
might blow truer of the storm and dew
and bay higher to the spattered sky
drawing with it my own.

Eve is thought to be unborn here
(where vacant lots run riot with wildflowers
and bottles are either not broken

or soon covered by the hills
      crawling
          silently
              down
on pilgrimage to the brown god)

but lacks only the age,
for a child   someday
      maybe
five years or fifty,
when my seed or those whom
I have touched and somewhat taken
christen "Eve"   for Becky
is nearly gone too
because of the age.

Painter's Lullaby

High on a ladder,
lugging the long midday heat
and earth calling from the battlement
to press headlong my ear to her song,
the first urgings inviting response
as a dominant note calls a tonic

as Hendrix' love for a guitar
created his early passing
when it knew no cradlesong
so sweet as the needle.

But I will be a painter not a musician,
stopping my ears with dirt and caulk,
for the grass cries "soon"
from the ground as it croons
just below me.

Casey Jones loved a great machine
and bled upon it as it sang to him,
for it knew no lullaby.

And the ladder sings me
up and down   and on
to the close of the day.

And though John Henry sang,
it was his own song in the wealth of his blood,
and when he was breathless
from sweating and singing
and swinging his mall,
he too bled upon the rails and died.

The groundsong will not be drowned
in paint or painter's sweat,
and each chip as it falls singing
sings to me.

I am only a hireling painter,
but I too have a song
and my song is a woman,

and when I settle with her,
it will be for her lullaby
settling me after the day
to her pulse playing through my veins

and when I leave for my ladders
it will be to sing the eyes and soul of her,
and to await her lullaby.

Songs of Hannibal

If Ever (Reflections on the Death of My Grandfather)

If ever when the tides of years have gone
And purplish-tinted evenings lose their glow,
If ever you should view the waking morn
Alone and think on times before I had to go,

Forbid this time, oh most benign,
You know the chill of loneliness.
You would not leave my dearest here
To dote on one enjoying bliss

Rather let us go as one,
Two lovers' souls to see your sun
Together—or leave me awhile
To wait, still wearing lover's smile.

But if the time must come with years
That sees my lover walk in tears
Remembering the enchanted life we had,
Then darling I'll not think you bad

If by some wisdom ages bring,
You put an end to everything
That I in happy times saw fit
to put in writing—lover's wit, and caring for,

And passion, yea
I urge you while I yet can say
That if this time must come to pass
Please burn my notes and rest at last.

Forgetfulness is bliss they say
While loneliness remains a prey
To sorrow, and wretched tears
Ah, memories of those happy years!

But I above will wait on you
And know that yet your love is true
And while I drink ambrosial toasts
I'll know your burning of my notes

Is just to quiet love of ghosts.

To A Not So Wee Wasp In Waiting

Peace, you twit!
I've only come to paint my house,
      not yours
although it seems that yours is mine also,
built as it is on mine.

Or do wasps have squatter's rights?
I think they must
      but not where it is inconvenient.
And yes I've heard that a wasp's home
      is her hive,
and that is why you must move.

Take also your brood,
since I'll not be responsible
for their proper upbringing
nor will I have them clinging
to my neck and you screaming: BRUTE!

I'd rather ease you out now,
spray you dead without their seeing,
spray mute the silos
preventing their fleeing,

I will
though I'll feel like Herod.

Under Their Wings

As an exceptionally clueless young teen,
Receiving all the favors paid to youth
Of many persons' acts of charity
Supporting me, some secretly,
In countless quiet self-effacing ways
So much generosity to me
Lavished freely by so many
Some of whom I didn't even know
Or knew my benefactors only
By their names or smiles
But never by their beneficial deeds
And still do not, up to this very day!
(Except of course my grandparents
And easy family friends.)

Remembered chief among the group
Of generous well-wishers

Of those I *knew* who gifted for my sake
Their time or talent, prayers for me,
Best wishes for a pleasant path in life
No hope of recognition or reward
Beyond the innocent warm glow
Resulting from the types of gifts they gave
Was a small but active coterie
Each unknown to the others
Whose names I well remember to this day
Who took me under their protective wings

The sweet and generous older girls
Who taught me how to kiss,
And practiced with me
When we had the chance.

"...the Great Mississippi, the majestic, the magnificent Mississippi, rolling its mile-wide tide along, shining in the sun."

~Mark Twain

Mississippi River Town (Autumn)

Returning ancient currents in the wind
Following the drawn out gluey summer,
Sifting clean the muzzling immigrant air
Weighted full with airborne prairie topsoil.

Gusts relieve the valley, sweep and sigh,
Coursing eddied whorls through yawning streets
Injecting timid spirits with sterner marrow
Passion and promises into the lungs of the young.

These mistrals wild as gales Ohio-borne
That gusted from the Alleghenies down
When white men first this Mississippi spied
And the freed second-born cried aloud

From the heart of the land.

ILASCO: a small town located "just a good stone's throw" downriver from Hannibal, built in large part by Eastern European immigrants (primarily from Poland, Italy, Hungary, the Ukraine, Romania, Croatia and Slovakia) who came to America for a better life, and virtually all of whom were employed by an enormous cement plant (now Continental Cement). The town's name is an acronym for the ingredients of cement: iron oxide, lime, alumina, silica, calcium sulfate and oxygen. Many of the descendants of these early immigrants still live in Ilasco today.

An Observance On the Wives of Ilasco
(ca. 1970)

Why
haggard mothers of hill-waifs
have you bought with your virginity
more toil than evening can erase
and bartered spinsterhood's lonely ease
to function resented as a man's ball and chain

is your chosen submission so love-lucrative
that tenderness rewards your breasts
finally hardened against the irreverent nips
            of your babes
and the entitled and sacrilegious brutalizing
            of your men
                    or
was the choice never made?

Joseph Welch

Lament of the Young Profligate

Wondering only
      how to explain
      something
to this stranger
      with the musky neck
      and belly
who lay beneath him

he ultimately
      confessed
that he could not afford
      to lose
another dream
      this summer.

"To love another person is to see the face of God."

— *Les Miserables*, Victor Hugo

First Glance

Oh, it was friendly… (I remember)—
You…bemused….
Me…astonished!

On first seeing you
Love leapt in me.
Stunned senseless,

I smiled and said EVERYTHING
I could manage:
(which was) "Hi."

And I remember
Just as you passed
(Me sniffing at your lashes)

I turned
And watched
Your bottom

And that fine
And full
Cascade of hair

Which flowed
And rippled
Darkly down your back.

You went away.

But the most remarkable thing—
The image frozen in time:
Your face

Mischievous
Young and fresh
Around two big dark eyes

Wide eyes
Doe eyes
Love eyes

Smiled!

(The scarcest whisper
Of a shadow…
Of a hope…
Of a promise…
Of delight.)

Joseph Welch

Kitten

I am not the poet
that you are the poem

this is obvious to me
who have been sitting here
for three and a half hours now

    trying to tell you something

all I wanted to say
something about kittens growing up to be cats
and something else about one who didn't:

    I love you.

Late Last Night

Late last night,
in the assurance
of another day lived,
and the regret of
another day gone,
I beheld clearly
my life-changing destiny!

I even mapped and plotted
all the efforts to achieve it,
resolving then and there
to start AT ONCE--
heedless of sweat and expenditure—
and personal cost be damned!

To recreate myself
in the image of my vision,
a wondrous metamorphosis,
transformed and born anew,

a beacon and example
to myself, not least of all,
clothed henceforth in my
splendid colors true—

All resolutions, by the by,
which I most earnestly
then vowed to keep.

But this morning's
early sparrows
laughed at me asleep.

Joseph Welch

A Question

What type of woman
drinks wide-eyed and willing
from the vanishing cup
of our time

rising early
(for I am a man
of many habits—
and intense)

to rid the room entirely
of the night's license
knowing even as she
last night moved with me

that Ovid's volume
placed open on the desk
would shrive
my morning soul.

My Muse

Yes, I've seen her,
my enabling muse
very female, of course,
which fact is hardly lost on me.
She uses it shamelessly
to inspire me,
draw out my ardency,
lay bare my offerings.

Soft! Her beauty sings to me.
I see and know her.

I am naked and eager
and unafraid.

Joseph Welch

The Unspoken Thoughts of My Bride

Deep, surpassing deep
Profoundly inscrutably deep
Pondering quietly deep in her heart
Secret and silent oracle
The unspoken thoughts of my bride.

Bride Psalm

Bride of the liveliest wit
Bride of the tender heart
Bride of the soulful eyes
Bride of unceasing affection
Bride of my most ardent longing
Bride servant of the true God.

Joseph Welch

Night Mare

Fit   shockingly fit!
Strong as the neck of a mare
Taut belly and sinewy haunches
When first I knew you
Mare of my night riding.

Nimble and shapely and silken
And sleek your legs and mane
And sweet your compliance with capture
Your calm wide-eyed animal gaze
Breathed fragrant invitation.

Your symmetry soft as caresses
Your beauty encouraged my kisses
Your sumptuous lips led to nurturing gifts
In my hopeful dreams scarcely imagined
Our imminent beautiful children.

Evening Sky (Late March)

Ebbing of the second day of spring
Evening's awning shades the land from light
Sky-borne currents, tufted golden rims
Stream across the dusking trackless deep.

Bright-lined nimbus flagships of the daysky
Fade to drifting gray titanic bergs
Legions without number tramping onward
Soundless to their obscure destiny.

And under all the backyard bat
Plies his ancient kiting trade
Flutters in the fresh night-shade
Veers and hovers, tracking prey.

Lightning flashes twenty miles away
An early small mosquito lands to feed
Wind suckles drizzle from a pregnant cloud
And spilt rain slaps across my upturned cheek.

Of what significance are we
Among all this—except we see,
Our vista but a particle of earth
And earth itself a smidgen of the sky

But coming here with one I love we might
Lie together close and pass the night
Watch together random orphaned stars
Roaming 'mid the vasty moonstacked swells

To see Orion's belt engulfed
Over-billowed, conquered, lost,
Half-moon sketches edges of the flume
Unimagined chasms shown ablaze.

To watch the sky unfurl in fits and streaks
And store this time away against our age.

My Favorite Mammal

I know a sweet soft glossy one,
A warm and supple and yielding one.
She flicks her tail and offers to play.

Fertile belly readies and waits—
Daring eyes consent, say
Have your way with me.

Other mammals have their devotees:
Lovers of figures and fur,
Markings and manes,
Haunches and whiskers and tails,

But had I not known you:

What would I now think
Of little Ms. Mouse
Who lays soft
In her downy nest
(So still)

Her small ones
Rooting and tugging,
Her mouse nipples
Leaking on her belly

Sweet pap
Flowing
In the mouths
Of her babes.

Akela Raksha Returns to the North

She senses it—our malamute,
Wayward bitch of the frozen north,
Northern Wisconsin born and bred,
To Missouri borne (not bred).

Once a year when the days grow long,
Attenuated by insect song,
Heat settles in, the drone of bees,
She waits for night, and cool and breeze.

Our restlessness and running 'round,
Our shouts, the packing of the van:
Our fishing poles, her water bowl,
She circles close and begs to go.

Do the northern skunks smell good
To you, Akela Raksha,
Lift from memory the shroud
That overlays your warm wet time?

Can you see from the past in your doggie mind
The birches of your puphood,
Your giant father's prodigious strength,
Your mother's welcoming belly?

Can you now, snuffling, recollect
The powerful dog fragrance
Of your early puppy nest
And all your tumbling siblings small again?

Joseph Welch

Concubine

Arise, bride of the spear

Your captor desires your beauty
Steppe-born woman of mystery
Limb-borne incense wafts from your bed
Steeped in the baths of your ancestors

Stretch for me, languid one
Enchant me, sweet artificer
Unfold, fresh flower
Display your concubine's heart

(For in your eyes flashes fire
Of such as pleased the Genghis Khan)
Bride of the short night, enfold me
Like the budcase on the rose, hold me

Your line will endure
Your beauty invites procreation
You extract a promise from your lord
To plant within you prince and princesses.

Lady Junco

On this gray wet mid-March day,
I watched from several feet away
behind my all-glass Treetop cottage wall,
a tiny female junco
pausing from her long migration
in the pouncing cold and livening Ozark wind,

to hunt for scrumptious morsels
in the promising detritus
of a hoary ancient balding rocky hill,
whose crumbling genuflection
paid obeisant obligation
to the universal god of gravity.

She-junco, perfect, small, hackberry gray,
scouting grit among the mottled stones,
crept over to a puny cedar slip
which dared to dare the mortal weather risk,
all caution thrown to ruling hillside winds,
the upstart slip as short as squatted squirrel

a mere handful of bitty branches tossed,
each bough waved wings in pomegranate hue
all finely feathered pins in perfect rows,
moved in toward her selection, found intriguing or enticing,
or only just presenting when she needed touch and rest,
or maybe by a special invitation from the sprout--

perhaps it sang in verdure-scented notes.
She stopped beneath one windblown waving shoot,
and first she paused and let it scratch her back,
consenting, while it felt and sniffed at her
as I might offer up a genial hand
in greeting to a dog I didn't know.

Assured then of its amiable arms
she stepped beneath the waving spray
of tiny pins and miniature boughs,
and peeked about inside the puny hut,
and found it fitted her proportionate
in size and shape sufficient to her need,

then fluffed her perfect cozy coverlet
and hunkered down to rest untroubled there,
while still she rode the slow hill's deathless crawl,
her bright black eyes fixed on the windy world.

Shescape

Soft…oh
soft as moon
down the gleaming
rise and fall of you

my wondergaze
all rapt in quiet awe
entranced by
lure of your allure

marvels at the elegance
of silky rounded slopes
and shapely vales
inclining down to love

and one distinctive furrow
overnested by its crested
glade and secretly
perfumed by freshet there

enchanted eyes stare mesmerized
to view your sculpted woman's back
merge in that wondrous
flaring of your hips

I see in solemn reverie
your image from prehistory
your gendercall to men like me
from time before time was.

Joseph Welch

From the End of the Lagoon

Again this somber raw November day
cast on the lake a gray and godly sheet
clear windbreath sighing trackless trails of scent
mumbles and hums in insubstantial song
piling sodden spillages of cloud
into layers of slow pearlescent iron.
The ashen ancient land unglutted still
by weary weight of blood and fur and bone
eternal unrelenting thirst unslaked
adores the benefactress god
while nursing stunned and wide-eyed
as the shapely nourishing ripples,
symmetrical, pewterine, perfect
roll softly, softly into the lagoon.

Deer

Dusky deer family
sealed snug and tweedy
under our great white pine
fantastic ears in silhouette
doe eyes wide as flight
fixed on the sight of me
watching them watch
still as coiled springs
the timeless and motionless
wary patience of prey.

Then finally assured
turn slender heads
to the tender tips
to sample our sentinel pine.

Can they possibly think
that our pine tree
is actually theirs?
(Or maybe just these tips, hmmmm?)

What must it feel like
to claim only
what you can nibble?

September Morning (The Deck)

Under a lightening gossamer dawn-trailing sky
And then the slow-motion outburst of daybreak just past
Now bathed in a sensuous runnel of God's gentle breath
And watching our yard, a spontaneous theatre of life,
Play out in torrents of green and spillover gold.

Mercurial hummingbirds dart in and hover to feed
Oblivious squirrels sport heedless on runaway paths
Along lofty reaches of redbud and tulip and cherry
Hackberry, hemlock and walnut, our transplanted oak
Our bountiful skyline trees that we well know and love.

A squirrel stops to perch and wag and taunt
(But whom, we fear we'll never really know)
Birds glide and dive in pairs and companies
While whiffs of lace-vine lightly float the breeze.

In the center of this quiet bedlam and next to me: You.

Amidst all of this morning madness, I see only You.

Sipping your first fragrant coffee, your dark eyes alight
Observant, aware, nearly awed, still too early to watch
For your recent most curious friend, the insistent bee,
And wearing your glorious rich-rumpled good-morning
hair,

Amid the overlaying, intoxicating, unaccountable,
So perceptible, pure delectable, yummy and insistent

Scent of lovely you.

God is love.
And he who abides in love
Abides in God
And God in him.

$\qquad$ 1 John 4:16

I Could Never

Shit. Piss.
The boy fell in the mud.
There—I've done it.

Told the underside. For balance.
Glad that's over—come, Love—
Now I can reflect on Truth and Beauty.

I could never write a novel.
All my characters would have to be good
And honest, or at least honorable.

And all the women captivating
Pure of mind, but free of heart--
Generous.

Because I could never create
Someone less than perfect.
How does God do it?

Can it be even possible that we are perfect
Just as we are, just *because* we are?
I could never know the mind of God.

So little that I understand
And what I know is often wrong.
However, I still hope to use my gifts:

To lend worshipful caresses, say,
To help some insubstantial way
Assisting in the endless cosmic quiver.

Cedar Ode

Legions of Eastern Red Cedars,
bevies of plump Rubens beauties
whose maxim is merely to thrive,
defying the rules for planting
(thou shalt not sow rocky ground
nor nonexistent topsoil
nor where the weeds may choke)
for even meager clay supports lush growth.

No need to carry water during drought
or guard against most common pests
such as that nemesis of evergreens
the fierce and dreaded bagworm;
stout enough to fend off rampant vines
ivy, grape, euonymus, briars and creepers.

Opportunely populating fissures--
a seam in local limestone
lacking soil, formed eons past
by bony husks of ancient marine life
provides a cedar's comfy bed and board;
the dizzy sides of sheer rock bluffs
with cedars are adorned on tiny ledges
too desolate for even grass to grow.

Dark blue fruit invites perpetuation
by partner namesake cedar waxwing birds--
and a few such gnarly twisted trunks
in quiet worship, kneeling,
and wedged in barren ageless living rock
prevail against the wind a thousand years.

Joseph Welch

Let Us Drink Also

Empty of other thought and dream and heed
while dumb and muffled surging night surrounds
such plaintive and relentless beggar need
to bargain brute bepearled nightly sounds
senseless eruptions from the minds of men
for the sleeky silken vision
of that god that woman is.

Propter dona misericordiae tuae
humilibus famulis tuis
(For the gifts of your mercy
to your humble servants)
we yearn again, and still.

Let us drink also the fragrant
incarnal knowledge of your mind,
nursing in our endless searching need
from your eyes as we gaze without fill,
from your breasts as we gorge without glut.

Joseph Welch

Our Treetops in Winter

Entranced by our swaying winter skyline
random grouped bouquets of fingerlings
each species recognized and known to us,
now unadorned, penciled in, visibly distinct,
outlined against a surly winter sky
each thin shoot the summit of a branch
the prior leafy season's reach of growth.

The stretching of their twiggy tips
supplicants for sustenance
water from the airy sky
dreams of fountains gushing light
balmy wished-for talismans
against the steady wind and ice,

enduring with the pain of passing time.

Do they dare to contemplate
a slow deciduous hope
that an expected second coming
brings again their sap flow singing
and the crowning fresh green
promise of new spring?

But perhaps there is
no hope or expectation—
perhaps they only reach
in adoration.

"The years like great black oxen tread the world,
And God, the herdsman, goads them on behind,
And I am broken by their passing feet."

> ~*The Countess Cathleen,*
> *William Butler Yeats*

Reminiscence

Young and overcome with vasty night,
Or scent of spring or ancient autumn new,
A vista, or the sea, or some fine girl,
A midnight run across a darkened bridge,
Or coming home fresh-bloodied from a fight,
Or savagely exulting on a hill,
Embracing longed-for fresh auspicious winds,

Have I ventured strong and strange
With my mustang stallion heart
Into open welcome free familiar sport.

But now I shamble all alone
Through some decayed and painted port,
Recreating splendid not-forgotten scenes,
Reflections in my dim and aged mind,
Knowing equal feats will never be--
Though they were fairly dazzling at the time,
I paid a price--look what they left of me.

Childbride

You were just a child
when first I knew you
a stunning child of
perfect and surpassing
beauty
and innocence
a mirthful child
enormous eyes missed nothing

But omigod
my heart was drawn to you
in pain and hunger
squeezed and twisted
wrung out
mangled for want of you
a beggar for your beauty
stunned in your presence
obsessive in your absence
struggling not to show
the obscene depth
of my need

Let me not now
begin to list your
catalogue of charms
but don't think
that I don't
remember them

it's only that
my memory
explicit and complete
may be much
too much
to so describe
your features oh so
memorable to me

And just because
I will not here and now
compile and itemize
your perfect girlhood
mind and body
your angel dreams
and parts and places

recall of which can
make a grown man weep
does not mean I forget them
oh my love

Let me not now
even summon up
your overwhelming
girlhood loveliness
my mind tumescent
with recollection
I may never sleep again.

Songs of Hannibal

Once I Was A Young Man

Once I was a young man
On a vague but pressing quest
Imagining all sorts of lovely things

And you were there--
Unmet as yet,
A spirit in my dreams.

Like patterns on the water
Or illusions in the clouds
Or whispers that were not quite overheard,

Or music in the background
Just beyond my conscious thought,
Desperate, in eagerness I searched.

Your image formed in vagaries
Of delicate allure
That I could never wholly apprehend,

Yet still I hoped and longed for you
My aspirations led to you
I knew that even nameless, you were there.

I was certain I would know you at first sight,
That somehow I would recognize you then.
Saved by faith and hope and love (I swear)

That instantly, with your first glance,
I felt your fresh suffusion
Of all that built within me fledged anew

Of that which set my orbit
Square beneath those spangled stars
That I then beheld and longed to share with you.

Daybreak

It was a time like any other.
Grey pearl light arrived,
Huddled at the edge of the world
And breathed on the night
And blew out stars
And covered the moon.
Unbeaten wind grazed on the earth
And animals roused and stretched and shook
And the high pale sky streaked
And birds called to the travelers:
Another day.

The man walked toward the open door
Out among the flocks
And nodded to the knot of men
Who stared from places at the fire
Then moved away to urinate.

Still inside, sufficient for the moment,
Amid the tang of sweet hay
And steaming beasts and dung,
A young girl lay warm in her robes
And opened her eyes, and stared
And wondered that the times required it:
A world away from home
No family knew
Nor neighbor women up and fixing food
Or treading well-marked places to the well
That Mary had her baby.

Joseph Welch

The Puppy Puppy Pomes

The Puppy Puppy Pomes

Some years ago, one of our children came home from school reporting that a certain little boy had earned the dubious distinction of additional scrutiny due to his habit during recess of chasing the little girls around the playground and trying to kiss them while peppering them with the singular entreaty: "Puppy, puppy!" This image soon caused these words to take on fresh meaning to my wife and me. The *Puppy Puppy Pomes* (largely written as Valentines) are the result of this historical phenomenon.

"It may be only puppy love, but *have you seen my puppy?*"

~JW

Joseph Welch

Puppy Love

I have a little puppy that I dearly love to see
And all the scent and sight of her is such a treat for me!
She followed me to bed last night
(She snuggles very sweet!)
All day I think of cuddling her—
I hope we can repeat!

I have a little puppy who goes out to play with me--
The cutest little puppy that my eyes will ever see!
I like my little puppy friend;
I want for her the best:
Of love and health and exercise
And puppy happiness.

I have a little puppy who will sit down on my knee.
I love to tell her stories and to set her spirit free.
I long to lie and pet with her
And while away the time,
And snoof and kiss and look at her:
My puppy Valentine.

~An Ardent Admirer

O Sweet Bewhiskered

O sweet bewhiskered
      puppy
            your eyes
reflect your
ancient
      ongoing
            intimacy

with man and woman
and the emulated child

for a long-time-longer
than thirty thousands of years

now the covetous claws of
nippy
      vicious
            mongrel
                carnal
                    curs
clutch at your sleek splendor

and even your
naughty kennel-mate
tries to make
puppies with you(!)

while acquisitive
self-appointed Fruitful Increasers
and Multipliers desire
Dominion over you

with Master's rules:
("good doggie" "bad!")
seeking to "train you up"
to scheduled adoration

but forgiving all
in your boundless friskiness
you respond with only
your pure and peerless
puppy self.

Snuggling With My Puppy

Snuggling with my puppy
With my soft warm puppy puppy
Wrapped around her curvy
Curly puppy tail.

This is one way that my puppy
My delicious puppy puppy
Makes her growly doggy
Lover truly male.

My entreating doggie whispers
In her soft warm puppy ear
'Mid the sweet and fine waftessence
Of her glorious she-fur.

Oh, my darling puppy puppy
Beg your pardon, puppy puppy
But our yummy puppy snuggling's
Almost more that I can bear!

God-cast puppy picture!
Who on earth can blame or stricture
When the Puppy-Maker tasks me
Making puppies, puppy love.

O Puppy Girl with Puppy Grace

O Puppy Girl with puppy grace
I loof to snoof your puppy face
O Puppy Girl my little miss
I dream of your sweet kiss.

O Puppy Girl consent to me
And let me be your puppy-he
I love your scent and love you too
I long to be with you.

She's the Sweetest Puppy Puppy

She's the sweetest puppy puppy
That my eyes could ever see.
And I would like to be with her
And have her be with me.

I want to kiss her puppy nose
And hold her in my arms
And touch her silky puppy fur
And pet her puppy charms.

I followed her to school one day
Her love light in my eyes
And following my puppy
Led to quite a nice surprise!

She's all that I can think about
My puppy and her charm
I couldn't help but follow
When she went into her dorm.

And now my puppy comes to me
And lets me hold her so
And my sweetest puppy puppy
Hardly ever tells me no.

My puppy puppy puppy
Keeps me fully occupied--
I love to play her puppy games
And watch her puppy eyes.

I love my puppy puppy so
I love her puppy way;
I love her sweetest puppy scent
When tumbling in the hay.

And when my puppy lies with me
Without her puppy clothes
I hope my puppy puppy
Always comes and never goes.

~ A Puppy Lover

O Wot Sweet Puppy Puppy*

(*To be read wearing a mustache and a Panama hat)

O wot sweet puppy puppy
Can I say sweet puppy puppy
That begins sweet puppy puppy
To explain

How I loav my puppy puppy
Loav to C my puppy puppy
Loav to kees my puppy puppy
And exclaim

O my pretty puppy puppy!
Willyustay sweet puppy puppy?
Willyubee my puppy puppy--
Please be mine!

And especially my puppy
My sweet big eyed puppy puppy
Willyubee my puppy puppy
Valentine?

Why Michael Wears Glasses

(according to brother Joseph)

I'm sure you all realize that our brother Michael wasn't born with glasses, but I don't know if you realize how he came to wear them. When he was young, his eyesight was perfect. He was possessed of extremely large orbs which his eye sockets could scarcely contain. His peripheral vision was fantastic. Michael's perfect eyes were a gift from God.

One Christmas season, my older brother John and I became concerned because our younger brother and protectee, Michael, had come up with the strange notion that there was no Santa Claus. To this day, we don't know where he got such an idea, whether it came from bad companions, or simply his youthful curiosity coupled with the inability to explain the wonder of it all. He started professing this new-found lack of belief to John and me.

Our attempts to set Michael straight only infuriated him. Perhaps some of you have witnessed how a great diver performs a "jack-knife" by elevating vertically off the board and, at the apex of the dive, in that precise moment when he hangs suspended between rising and falling, bends gracefully from the waist and touches his toes, before accelerating downward, headfirst into the water. Michael had this sense of timing and body control ability, but he put it to a slightly different use. He had developed his own "move"—he had perfected the ability to leap straight up into the air while bringing his knees up to his shoulder level just at the peak of his elevation, a "lock and load" maneuver designed to enable him to slam his feet down on the floor at the moment of his landing, thus exponentially increasing the room-shaking effect of his vault. It was nothing short of impressive. At the apex of this vertical display, Michael's face became beet red, he threw his head back and yelled defiantly, **"I'LL SHOW YOU!"**

Now Michael was a scientist. In order to prove his theory, he devised a simple experiment so diabolical in nature and efficient in operation as to take one's breath away. He procured a piece of paper and a clean envelope, upon which he wrote a note to the following effect:

"Santa, if you are real, please leave Mommy and Daddy $100 each."

Incredible! The sum was unheard of in my worldly experience—it existed only in the Land of Let's Pretend. He might as well have said a million dollars. Only Santa Claus could produce money with two zeroes behind it on our living room floor.

The letter was an extortion note addressed to his faith in childhood.

Michael's eyes became slits as he proofread this epistle and then penciled his name, without so much as the benefit of a complimentary closing. He folded the paper into eighths, stuffed it into the envelope, scrawled "Santa" on the front, and slid the entire device, like a landmine, underneath the corner of the living room rug.

John and I, who had been watching, horrified, unable to save Michael from himself, were helpless to deter him. We could and did, however, report the entire sequence of events to both Mom and Dad. Mom raised her eyebrows and said, "Oh?" Dad's face broke into a funny smile as he said casually, "Is that so?" It seemed to John and me that he didn't fully appreciate the gravity of the situation. Nothing else was said to relieve our worry over our fallen brother.

On Christmas morning, while the rest of us bolted excitedly to our piles of toys, Michael ran straight to "the spot" upon which his proof depended. He pulled out the envelope with his left hand and immediately snatched the contents out with his right. Then it happened: his eyes bugged clear out of his sockets.

I can still see him kneeling there on the floor beside the Oriental rug, holding up his folded pencil note with two $100 bills, his mouth half open, and his eyelids peeled back from those gigantic orbs as he sat, frozen in time, while the enormity of the event washed over him. He had been suddenly cast adrift from his newly found agnosticism. His eyes were locked and frozen, strained out from his sockets nearly to the tip of his nose. It was in this position that Mom and Dad, standing in the big double doorway several feet away from either side of him, found him.

Dad said, "What do you have there, Michael?" Michael, still holding the money at arm's length in front of him, rose as if in a stupor toward Dad and said, "Uh, I asked Santa Claus to bring you some money and he did." Dad said, "All for me?", to which Michael replied, "A hundred dollars of it is for you and a hundred dollars is for Mommy." Mom said, "Oh, Michael, that was so nice of you," and gave him a kiss as she took the proffered $100 bill from Michael's offering hand, then gave it to Dad "to keep in a safe place."

Michael's eyes were never the same after this event. Perhaps, if we had known, we could have massaged them or applied hot or cold compresses or given him lid relaxants, but we didn't know. We didn't realize until later that the damage had been done. Shortly thereafter, Michael began wearing glasses, which he wears to this day.

As it is for many of us, Michael's search for faith was at great personal cost. However, the entire event nonetheless blessed Michael with an understanding that could not be shaken by those ignorant boys and girls of the world who insisted on advancing a theory which Michael had already blown to hell.

Torching the Car

(ca. 1966)

Heading into the 57th year after the event, and having been assured that the Statute of Limitations has long run, this seems like the proper opportunity to tell the whole truth about an amazing event which occurred when I was a young teenager (age ~13). I have never told this to my own children because I didn't want to give them any bad ideas. However, since I now believe that they are old enough to deal appropriately with the historical record, I will break my silence of nearly six decades and relate the facts as I remember them.

First, however, it is necessary to set the scene: During my youth, I was possessed of pyromaniac tendencies, which I exercised as an outlet for my natural creativity. I was fascinated by the act of smoking—it just looked to me like some kind of magic. Once I stole a handful of Dad's pipe tobacco from its humidor atop the white cabinet beside our kitchen doorway, wrapped it up as tightly as I could in a strip of the colored Sunday "funny paper," sealed the homemade "cigar" with scotch tape, and took it surreptitiously to my bedroom to smoke. I lit the end with a couple of matches and was avidly puffing on it when I heard Mom approach through the hallway. I immediately tossed the entire assembly into the bedroom closet and slammed the door. When Mom came in and announced that she smelled smoke, I immediately replied, quite truthfully, with a contrite and confessionary air, that I had in fact been "playing with matches," (one of our "bringing up" phrases denoting *verboten* behavior). She gave me a funny look, taken aback I suppose by my very ready confession, (a desperation move--I needed her out of there pronto! I was experiencing intense visions of flames bursting through the closet door at her back). Looking thoughtful, she merely said "Oh," and left. As soon as she vanished from sight, I immediately raced over to the closet, opened the door, and stomped out the fallen "cigar" before I burned the house down.

I had also watched the "Big Boys" in the neighborhood, who fashioned pistols out of spring clothespins and rubber bands, which they used to fire wooden kitchen matches at one another in games of "war." The matches ignited as they exited the teeth of the clothespin "guns," and went smoking through the air like rockets. Some of the "Big Boys" actually had burn holes on their shirts where they had been "shot" with the flaming matches! How cool was that! However, to our bitter disappointment, we were never allowed to participate in this exciting game.

And then there was David Dye, an older boy who picked up his newspapers at the Market Street Fire Station, where my older brother John and I picked up the papers for our own routes. David Dye was a rocket maker and bomb assembler *extraordinaire*. He had a penchant for describing the huge craters left in the ground, excavated by explosions from bombs and rockets which he manufactured himself with potassium chromate, which he mixed with powdered sugar as an oxidant. Each day he would describe in graphic detail, his eyes glowing while he gesticulated wildly, the various explosives which he had ignited in his neighborhood.

My own paper route started at Collins and Summit Street and ran west along the Grace Street ridgetop, past our house, up North Division, then on a path through the woods to the top of North Griffith, North 20th, and Kingshighway. Dooley's Market was smack-dab in the middle. In those days you could buy a huge box of kitchen matches for ten cents, and I was always armed. I kept my box in my paper bag, and tossed them as I went along the route, like little daggers that burst into flame on impact with a passing wall, concrete steps, or the sidewalk. You could get a lot of "bang" for ten cents in those days.

It is against this backdrop of continuous pyrotechnic experimentation that our story unfolds. I know I was 13 or

14 years old, because I got my own paper route on Grace Street when I was in the 7th grade. Consequently, it was approximately 1966, and a hot early summer Saturday afternoon at 120 N. Griffith Street. Dad was home from work, Mom and Dad were safely ensconced in the house, and the Welch boys, with a group of other boys from the neighborhood, were playing Indian Ball in the street.

Most of the neighbors moved their cars when we played Indian Ball, but we didn't have to. Our car was parked beside our side steps, pointed east on Grace Street, next to the expansion joint in the street which constituted "home plate." In Indian Ball there was no pitching and no base-running, just batting and fielding, much like playing pop-up. In addition, there is no pitcher, so the batter simply tosses the ball up in the air with the bat shouldered, and then swings away. We stood in the center of the street and our car was parked against the curb next to us, so there was little danger of hitting the car. While the batter took his turn, his teammates generally milled about behind "home plate."

We had a brand new Plymouth station wagon, delivered fresh from the factory, and it was a beauty. The car still **smelled** new. It was an enormous white luxury wagon with a huge V-8 engine, a push-button transmission on the dash, and seating for nine. The back-facing third seat was accessed from the tailgate, after lowering the electric power window with a key from the outside or a button from the inside.

Dad had just "gassed up" the car and come home at noon. It sat, sleek and brilliant white in the summer sun, facing up the Grace Street incline. As I waited for my turn at bat, I noticed that gasoline was dripping from the gas cap hatch, since the tank was completely full and the vehicle was parked on an incline. The gasoline ran down the back fender of the car, splashed onto the pavement, then narrowed to a stream next to the curb, where it flowed downhill and west to the Griffith Street intersection, and then broadened into a graceful sweep around the corner to run south down the steep hill toward Broadway.

As I waited impatiently for my turn at bat, the opportunities presented by untended gasoline seeped into my fevered brain. Now, I wasn't about to just walk up and light our new car—I was not, after all, a **complete idiot**. I would choose a more remote location to observe the conflagration of fresh gasoline, a place where no real damage could occur. Whoever heard of the street catching fire, after all?

I darted into the house and grabbed my trusty box of Diamond Kitchen Matches. Sneaking down the sidewalk under cover of our new car to the front of the house, I turned the corner and jumped down the steps into Griffith Street. I saw that the gasoline ran down almost to the Morawitz house (our next-door neighbor) in a stream five inches wide.

I stood for two seconds at the corner and surveyed the "line of fire" down Griffith Street, for I was by nature a **careful and prudent person,** despite my fascination with flames. No vehicle, person, tree or bush stood in the way. Excellent! "This will be quick and colorful," I thought.

I loped downhill to the Morawitz property line, opened the box, selected my weapon, struck it on the side of the box, and dropped it at the end of the gas stream next to the curb.

The effect was dramatic. A streak of white-orange fire shot north up Griffith Street. Approximately three-thousandths of a second later, it accelerated through the wide graceful sweep of the curb on the corner of Griffith and Grace, and headed east *out of sight!*

Stunned, I ran up the steep hill to the intersection as fast as my feet would carry me and rounded the corner onto Grace. From that vantage, the only evidence of the passage of the flame up the street was a black smoking trail, and it appeared to be largely over with, except for a small pool of blue flame licking the pavement at the back of our new car, which I hoped to quickly stomp out.

As I ran alongside the charred curbing up Grace Street toward the car, however, my eyes focused on the reason for the existence of the remaining pool of fire. Gasoline continued to drip down in droplets from the rear of the car!

As I ran closer, I distinctly saw the gasoline droplets bursting into flame in mid-air as they fell off the back fender. Hurrying toward the car, I witnessed, to my utter horror, the fire actually **leap up** from droplet to droplet in mid-air, causing volleyball-sized fireballs as each drop ignited. Just as I arrived, the side of the car erupted into flames a foot high.

At this point, I knew the situation was out of control. I ran into the house, along with several of my brothers, yelling, **"Mom and Dad, quick! The car is on fire!"** I could hear one of my brothers, who had preceded me into the interior of the house, yelling, **"Dad, move the car!"**

Dad ran out the back door with his car keys in his hand. I tried to stop him, yelling **"It's too late—it's already on fire!"** As we reached the midway point between the back door and Grace Street, the entire car suddenly *torched.* With a horrendous roar, a tower of flame of Biblical proportions erupted from the gas cap. At forty feet above Grace Street, it made a transition from white flame to hot gases wavering against the sky, converting our new car into an enormous Bunsen burner.

At the moment of eruption, Dad was arrested in mid-flight, the rest of us in his wake. All arms went up involuntarily in front of our faces and we started backing into the house, still looking at the awesome spectacle in front of us.

Mom met us at the screen door. I'm not sure how much she had been able to piece together at this point, but her eyes were like daggers. "Go to your room," she said. I scurried in quickly, but as I ran into the room with Mom behind me and parted the sea-green checked curtains which she had made for us, I was absolutely horrified to find myself staring through the glass at the huge tower of flame which emitted from the back of the car only fifteen feet away from my window. I recoiled instantly.

"It's too close!" I yelled to Mom in the bedroom doorway. Saying nothing, she crossed the room to the bedroom window, parted the curtains, and was greeted by the same conflagration. She immediately recoiled. "You're right," she said, "It **is** too close—go to the living room, all of you."

The rest is a blur. The firemen came interminably slowly, the huge truck laboring up Griffith Street. The enormous torch continued unabated while the firemen directed hoses onto the car in an attempt to cool the gas tank and keep it from exploding. They made several forays toward the base of the torch with huge foam fire extinguishers, but it was too hot to let them get in close enough. Once they were interrupted with a huge **"BOOM!"** as the windows were blown out of the car, no doubt causing them to believe that they had just exited the land of the living. One of the firemen was dropped by the shotgun-like particles of sharp glass.

Eventually, however, a fireman, supported by two cooling hoses, was able to get close enough to foam the base of the fire. The torch vanished, and they foamed the entire car, inside, outside and underneath.

They stayed on for a couple of hours, making sure that the fire was completely out, picking up hoses and equipment, and tending their wounded. As I looked out the window at the charred black hulk of our new car, with the interior completely melted into goo, I had the sinking feeling that I was in trouble beyond my ability to extricate myself. Mom and Dad didn't punish me immediately, however, because there was so much activity, what with treating the firemen for injuries and dealing with the enormous crowd which had come running on foot from the four corners of the earth. I was in deep despair.

At this point, I turned to God. Suddenly, I knew what to do: it was Saturday, and confessions were being heard three blocks away at Blessed Sacrament Church. Even though I knew that the tragedy was not technically a sin, since sin requires an intent to do harm, I felt compelled to go.

"I need to go to confession," I announced hopefully. Mom and Dad concurred—I think it completely took the wind out of their sails as far as deciding what might be a fitting punishment for me. In fact, in spite of the enormity of my transgression (easily a 25 on a scale of 1 to 10) and the complete loss of our beautiful new car, I don't think Mom and Dad ever punished me at all or even talked to me about punishment for my stupidity. I did, however, learn a valuable lesson about gasoline which has stuck to me to this day--it scares me to death.

Dad walked with me down Grace Street on my way to confession. You could have cut the silence with a knife, until Mr. Golden yelled down to Dad from his porch on the high side of Grace Street as we passed: "Hey, Bob, got a car to sell?" I could have crawled into a hole. I was both surprised and proud of my Dad, however, when, without missing a stride, he responded immediately: "I'll trade you even."

Remembering Christmas Morning

120 N. Griffith Street, Hannibal
(ca. 1958-1970)

I would be hard pressed to conjure up a happier memory than the Christmas mornings of my Hannibal boyhood. The night before, instead of the usual pre-bedtime bounce on our Daddy's lap accompanied by his singing "boomp-boomp-dittum-dottum-wottum-choo," followed by his blessing on our foreheads, we had the family prayers and singing of carols, and finally, kneeling *en masse* in front of the miniature manger scene at the foot of the Christmas tree where we all had a good view, the recital of the Christmas Novena, which I still remember verbatim:

Hail and blessed be the hour and the moment in which the Son of God was born of the most pure Virgin Mary, at midnight, in Bethlehem, in piercing cold. In that hour, vouchsafe, oh my God, to hear my prayer and grant my desire, through the merits of our savior, Jesus Christ, and of his Blessed Mother. Amen.

Having dispatched the tribute to both Baby Jesus and his mother, we then looked to more earthly considerations. Our appetite was considerably whetted by Dad's reading *The Night Before Christmas*, after which we inevitably delayed bedtime with a plea for "one last look at the Christmas angel" on top of our tree, a check of our stockings, and the note to Santa Claus, complete with our offering of milk and Mom's cowboy cookies. Then we were dispatched to bed, where, after Mom's "tucking in" and good night kiss, sleep eluded the six of us for hours.

Invariably, we spent a long Christmas Eve night, interspersed with checking the sky regularly for signs of Santa and the reindeer, thinking we heard the tinkle of jingle bells and the prancing and pawing of little hooves, and occasional quick peeks from the hallway door across the dining room and into the wonderful and mysterious shadows which peopled the living room with the promise of wonders yet unknown. Eventually, however, sleep overcame us.

We were drawn out of the abyss of nothingness by the sound of Mom blowing Great Grandma Ryan's Christmas horn, and vaulted out of bed to assemble in the back hallway. Mom made sure we all had on robes (and slippers, of course) and we waited impatiently while Mom and Dad turned on the Christmas lights. At the signal, we burst through the doorway and across the dining room. Even the fuzzy red electric Santa Claus glowing warmly in the dining room window failed to slow us down, as we were propelled onward toward the Christmas tree, tinsel shivering softly, and the angel glowing serenely from her perch on top. We approached the double doorway pell-mell, our horizons broadening out into a vast expanse of Christmas morning, the room filled with colorful displays of treasure. At the living room doorway our paths diverged, as each of us darted straight to our "pile" of gifts from the Jolly Old Elf (Santa never wrapped presents). We dropped to the floor, picking up toys, clothes, and books, and yelling to no one in particular, "I got a Popeye punching bag!" or "a book of poetry" or "a tool set with real tools!" or "a fountain pen!" or "a watch!" or "a wood-burning set!"

I well remember the Davey Crockett Christmas, when we got warm red Davey Crockett robes expertly crafted by Mrs. Claus' nimble fingers on her machine at the North Pole, together with coonskin caps and rifles, and lanterns that flashed red and green. These toys were a tremendous stimulus to my imagination and provided me with many hours of nearly unendurable adventure playing Davey Crockett and Mike Fink in the living room (which had somehow been converted into a river boat by the singular device of carrying in all the dining room chairs and placing them in a large oval to act as the boat rail.) All of our guns, rubber knives and miscellaneous armaments were stacked on the in-facing seats of the chairs, while a tiny desk table was placed in the middle as the center of operations. In those days, "wild Indians" were a problem; they attacked us frequently, and bears and gigantic snakes were also a continuous concern. We dispatched all comers.

I still remember my favorite Christmas gift. My "pile" that year was on the sofa, which at the time rested against the north living room wall. After briefly investigating most of my visible presents, I noticed for the first time a very large package wrapped in Christmas paper and resting on the couch. This in itself was unusual—I had never received a wrapped present from the Jolly Old Elf. Furthermore, one end of the wrapping paper was undone. I cautiously lifted an edge of the wrapping paper and discovered a box of birdseed. Yelling excitedly, I quickly dispatched the wrapping. (The sound must have been thunderous to the occupant of the package.) There, unveiled before my amazed eyes, was the most beautiful bird I have ever seen, before or since. He sat atop his perch in an elegant silver cage, a sight fit for the family of the Czar. He was the color of flame, gold and red-orange, and as sweet a creature as ever graced the bars of a cage. Although he was a canary, he was not much of a singer, perhaps due to the fact that the atmosphere in our home was a bit too frenetic to nurture his vocal abilities. But he was certainly gorgeous, and I loved him. In spite of Mom's various suggestions, there was only one possible name for him in my mind: "Tweety."

(In those days, two deaths were all there was in the world to mar my early childhood, both by assassins: John F. Kennedy, who died suddenly at the hands of Lee Harvey Oswald, and Tweety, who was snatched out of flight by the highly trained and lethal jaws of our resident killing machine: Prince, the Warrior Dog. I distinctly remember where I was when I learned that each of them had been killed.)

I can still remember one Christmas morning, after the initial toys and gifts frenzy, going over to the fuzzy lighted Santa perched on the windowsill, and craning my head to see the Star in the East. Although first light was slowly approaching, the Star was clearly visible, unmistakable in its clarity, shining down into our window on North Griffith Street.

As we grew older, our entire family walked to early Mass before we opened our presents. Although we were old enough to realize the "true meaning of Christmas," I have to admit that, during Mass, our thoughts would occasionally wander unbidden back to our living room, and the wonders that awaited us when we returned home.

By this time, Mom and Dad had acquired a large nativity scene, which they placed back against the shelter of the juniper bushes which lined our front foundation. Because the front yard was above street level surrounded by a wall, the nativity scene was almost at eye level. We placed white Christmas lights in the evergreen bushes above the nativity scene, like stars in the heavens. It was beautiful.

One year it started snowing on Christmas morning shortly before we left for early Mass, and we walked down Grace Street on the unshoveled sidewalks, in a half inch of virgin snow, leaving sixteen footprints behind us. As we returned home along Grace Street, we could see from a block away our white Christmas lights illuminating the snow cap which sat atop the bushes, providing an ethereal glow for the manger scene displayed quietly below. It was one of the most moving views I have ever seen.

To this day, except for the Christmas mornings of my own children, nothing has quite surpassed the thrill of Christmas morning at 120 N. Griffith Street. In fact, as I grew older, my occasional dreams of heaven echoed the circumstances which surrounded those happy times.